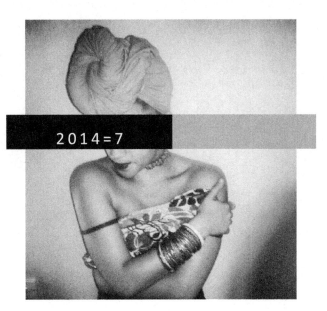

2014=7 | Chelsea R. Blues

Table of Content

- ∞ Introduction
- ∞ Poems of Reminiscing
  - ∞ Lost and found
  - ∞ Goddess to girl
  - ∞ Remembering
  - ∞ Chase
  - ∞ Tennis
  - ∞ First Half (Light side of the coin)
  - ∞ Second Half (Dark Side of the Coin)
- ∞ Poems of Self hate
  - ∞ Raspberry Cheesecake
  - ∞ Reprieve appeal
  - ∞ Five step tango
  - ∞ Skewed views
  - ∞ Flaws 101
  - ∞ Plea
  - ∞ Fairy
- ∞ Poems of Self love
  - ∞ Quiet Garden
  - ∞ Theatrical Love
  - ∞ Diana (I love me)
  - ∞ Notes To Me
  - ∞ Intra
  - ∞ One's Own Company
  - ∞ Trinity Being

INTRODUCTION

Poems of reminiscing

Lost and Found

If at some point
You find yourself at a cross road
And one can do this often –
Find themselves I mean –
Take time to review,
How you've reached thus far.

I tend to lose myself often.
To which me gets mad at I for.
Yet, every time I find myself,
I seem to gain a little each time.

So when I hit crossroads,
Railroads,
Dual carriage ways and all,
Looking back where me, myself and I
Travelled along,
Helps the decision forward,
For the best route along.

Goddess to Girl

Little strange girl
You run around all day
Daydreaming of successes
You'd one day be too afraid
To achieve

Little Strange Girl
You talk to the ocean and the sky
In all their glory
Outside your house on the Ridge.

You speak to them
In the language of fairies
Writing your poetry in a book
You'd lose and cry for
When you get older and full of self-hate
Looking for a reminder of better times

Little strange girl, You were
Always
Destined for greatness
If only you would have opened
Your eyes
Sooner

Little girl whose strangeness
Knows no limits
You are born of salt air
Warm wind
Baked sand
Seasalt bubble bath waters

You will leave it someday
to follow your heart's wishes

Little strange girl
You love flowers in your hair
You don't know it yet, but you always will.

Little strange girl
I am writing to you
You're now a strange woman, Quite beautiful too

Little strange girl
Who becomes strange woman
I am she,
The Psycho Goddess you grew up to be.

REMEMBERING

Looking back I remember
wanting to desperately stand out
in an accepted way, you know?
I remember being told
you can't have both
either you stand out
or you fit in
there's no two ways about it

I remember
dreaming
while wide awake
of worlds
I could never say out loud

I remember
seeing images of myself being hurt
by persons I trusted and loved
I knew would not

I remember
being called crazy
being hated by some boy
a grade or two below me –
for being too happy and weird.
I remember laughing
at him
and walking away

I remember
random things that
until today
I never understood.

Chase

He and his friend
Would run every recess
To be as far away from me
As they could possible

I would run after them
In mindless glee
Not know why I did
But content with the game

Some days I'd have a Vienne Sausage
The small ones mom packed for lunch
Then chase them screaming
'WEINER!'

Only God knows why I did it
Cause to me, it was funny
And that was a bad thing to say
But I said it anyways

One day while running behind them
They decided to stop

I never had a clue
What I was going to do if I caught them
So
I gave up that day, walked away
From Chase and his friend with the rosy cheeks.

TENNIS

I always wanted to play tennis
But I never got to play on the court

There was one time while leading a summer camp
That I learnt with the children I watched
How to play

Looking through an intense eight years of my life
I found that I played tennis quite often
Serving myself – as tennis ball –
Between my divorced parents

From Grand Turk to Nassau,
Nassau to Grand Turk,
Back to Nassau,
Nassau to Providenciales
Finally the game was called to a close
As this tennis ball had to remain in Nassau in the end

My parents – the mere players of the game –
Didn't see that I thought I was WonderWoman

My parents must have thought
I am a tennis player
An avid one too

Tossing myself
Side to side
Both the tennis player and the tennis ball
I ping-ponged my life.

First Half

Picture little me
I couldn't dance
I had rhythm – but my moves didn't stand a chance
They took me in
Taught me what I know

I was timid and quiet at home
Always cheerful and trusting though,
They taught me to watch my back
Stand up for myself too

They taught me how to dress
I must confess
I prefer comfort over style any day
Unkempt and unruly – much like my personality –
But that was fixed eventually

I was all talk and rarely any show,
They taught me, quite a few times actually,
Why action is better than spoken words

Watching and learning,
I saw why street smart was necessary,
Book smart just as so
To make a valid argument know your know,
To avoid the worst possible scenario,
While making your opponent look as stupid as they sound –
Not the other way around.

They taught me to be a go getter
You want it and people are saying no
You make it happen
Prove others wrong
If you can't be strong for yourself
No one else will
BOY that was a lesson to learn
I was a slow learner with that one

This is the first half of the coin
That the gods flipped for the fate of my life
Though I received tough love
There was much to be won

Second Half

Once upon a time
Early 2000's to be exact
A young girl would feel attacked

She would be beat up
Ostracized, played with,
Messed around with,
Not touched right...

She would try to please
Everyone at once
Only to disappoint everyone
Including herself

She would cut her skin
Skip classes
Refused, after school,
To go to her house of horrors before 5
Woke up upset every morning,
Fall asleep in tears

Her colour would bring her pain
Her hair always unmanageable
Her dreams ridiculed
Her grade always less than outstanding

Talked down to
Talked about
Used and abused
With words and trust

This is looking down only one side of the coin
Writing only what stood strongly in my memory.

Poems of Self Hate

Raspberry Cheesecake

In small doses you're harmless
Helpful even
Tantalizing my taste buds
Clouding my mind
Wearing a smile on my face
Knowing full well what you're doing to me

Attacking me from the inside
But I continue to eat
You begin to comment loudly on my figure
You cast me into a maze of verbal self-harm

Chanting out
Mmm's and Aaah's
As I take each treacherous bite
Enjoying the temporary pleasure
As I slowly
Self
Destruct.
It's not you; it's what I am allowing you to do.
It's my response to your version of love.

REPRIEVE APPEA

Can she be loved?

Lost

So far gone in a dream
That reality is passing her by
She let it all go by

How to tell her to get her head out of the clouds?

How to show her the truth of it all…

Blaming herself isn't the way
But, oh man,
Those clouds are so grey

Still wondering how to light her way
How to get through a rain cloud
Without coming out drenched

Five Step Tango

Breathe

Scream

Fight

Cry

Repeat

Do this all in your mind
Until you explode
And everyone thinks
You're seeking a bit of attention
Nothing more

Breathe
Scream
Fight
Cry
Repeat

Torture yourself
Beat yourself up
You were never good enough
Never will be
Why do you even bother
Wouldn't it be better
If you just
Happened
To die?

Breathe

But would your parents be okay? Would they cry?

Scream

It would cost them a fortune to bury you.

Fight

It won't matter no one will come to the funeral,
Don't forget they only like you for your color

Cry

That's what you've been told, no?

Breathe

Better stay alive and trod on.

Repeat.

Skewed views

I'm a good person
With good intentions
My actions seem not to reflect this
But, it's still true is it not?

I meant to buy you
A gift for the occasion
But I didn't have much money
It was you or my belly...

Although the truth is
I could have split it in half
Instead of spending it all on one dinner
With a friend
Because they asked
I could have said no
But I wanted to be there for them...

Maybe I'm not good after all

Worthless
To myself even
I should try harder
But trying doesn't
Really accomplish anything...

FLAW 101

Too fat
Too skinny
Too curvy
In all the wrong places

Bucked teeth
They're crooked also
Your legs are scared
So is your face
You pick at it
You've got backne
Pimples of your chest
You've got a moustache
Your leg and underarm hairs
Grow back too quick

Let's talk about the mountain
You call a forehead
And one day you'll have
Pretty hands – IF
You ever grow and respect your nails.

You tell yourself you can sing,
But you have no training – you're not THAT good yet.

You walk around too happy
People told you they hate that
You're too emotional
Too caring and touchy.

Fix everything about you
Then come back
We may have a wardrobe fit to hide the rest.

Don't let me be alone
When I am by myself
I have to tolerate
Being alone in my skin

I get to thinking
And Feeling
Overthinking
Reassessing
Putting on all of my clothes
So I can get rid of
The naked feelings

Answering to myself
Why have I locked love away?
Living heart hearted
Joy forever drifting

A wave of nausea hits me
I begin to feel dizzy
I don't want to
Face the mirror alone

Take me out
I will eat drink and dance
Sing for you like
The bells in a jewelry box
You open time and time again

I will find every excuse to
Be out and about
Not home
Not alone

Fairy

Small tiny hands of fairies
hug me as I cry in my sleep

Voices sing to me of

Something

Of this energy

Called love

But to me that was
Childsplay
Mere fantasy
Nothing more

How could one
Claim to love themselves
Don't we have to live with themselves

Why would you have to 'love' it...

These fairies seem to believe
That this life
Is worth it
They keep coaxing me on

One day my hatred may grow into a flower...

Until then – they hold me in my sleep

As tears betray my numb.

Poems of Self Love

Quiet Garden

Holding onto the faith
That's brought me to this place
Of quiet and peace
These calm waters inside of me

I consult the higher power within me
To go forth
Run my river of honesty
Into my daily being

Speak your mind
Speak it clearly
Reach the acceptance button
Apply it to yourself
Your way of being

Never let go
Of who you are
For temporary flight
Of 'joy'

Seek happiness within you
To carry through the journey
Grow to love every new aspect of yourself
Each day

Return to the inner goddess
To continually reaffirm your peace

Theatrical Love

Curtain rises. Person alone on stage.

An ode
A haiku
Maybe a ballad
A couplet – or two

Pours self a glass of wine

I have shown myself a kindness
I ate a piece of chocolate
Thanked myself for a change
Rather than beat myself up over it

So to celebrate this courageous act
towards a VIP
I have contemplated
various ways to show my gratitude

A poem

Not just a poem

A play

Not just a play

A skit in poetic rhythm
Starring the VIP of the last _____ years

They have put up with my bullshit
They have talked to me when there was no one else
Helped to drink me into pools of rum
Then swim out of the shark pit of hangovers
Hugged me tightly
to keep from breaking
When no one was around to see me cry

This person deserves an award
SO I am here to present just that

A toast
To loving me and I loving you
And by damn – that feels good.

Curtain fall

Diana (I love me)

What does self-love mean to you?

To me it was writing out
Everything I thought I knew about myself
Until I couldn't think of anything else

I'd then rip up the paper
As I didn't understand
What knowing these things really meant

I wrote down my the 'flaws'
People saw in me, so I thought I saw in myself
I wrote down my 'good' qualities
That I knew I had

One day I made a pact to myself
To forgive the people
For their lack of understanding
Then take every day
To fully understand and accept myself

To you my young one
Whom I love dearly
Look deep in the mirror
And repeat loudly

'I am what I make myself to be
Regardless of anyone or anything
I love me

All I have
Myself, my thought and spirit
No one else can bear my pains
As no one can cure them
I alone can allow it

Once again
I love me'

Notes To Me

Swirl and circle
Laugh and pout
You have freedom of expression
If you allow

Smile often in the mirror
Be honest with yourself
Be open to feeling down
Yet, don't stay there

Live wholeheartedly
Throw all of your efforts
Into that which inspires you
Things you love

Don't give 50% if you're expecting 100%
If you feel 10 express 7*
Enjoy it fully still

Feel free to create
Be open to change
Take life one day at a time
Be free and smart

Be your own joy card
Make the most of everything

Words to me from myself

---

*Anne Bogart

INTRA

Take a deep breath
Feel the hairs on your body raise
The goose bumps trail up your arms
Your heart beats rapidly
The exhilaration is intense

Head held high
Shoulders relaxed
You gulp
Lunge
Head first
Nothing to cling to
Just falling

Wind in your ears
You cannot hear it though
Smiles creep to your face
You can't help it
Or stop it, for that matter

Every movement
Every word
Every moment
Yours to own

You say, do, think, feel, express
Only the truth of you
This is a consistent free falling
Living and loving yourself wholeheartedly.

One's Own Company

Shutting off all devices
Going ghost
No FB,
Twitter
Tumblr
Nor Insta
Today I am taking the day off

I will not be ultra-available
I am cutting down my
24 hr call services
There will be no photographic evidence

I will not be easy to find
Unless you too take a walk
Hand in hand I'll be with myself
Today I'm treating me - no one else

Going to bed early the night before
I will rise when I wake.

Take a long bath
Reading my book with music
'll shave and wash my hair

Take my time to get ready
No rush to be anywhere
Shall I cook myself something,
Or eat out instead?

Buy myself a bottle of wine ...
Rum
Sounds more like it.
And take myself on a picnic

Then return home strip myself bare
Turn on my heater then write poetry in bed
Read the rest of my book
Watch a movie or two
Sleep for the night

Tomorrow my devices will be on

Tomorrow you can reach me again

Trinity Being

Using this body
But not really living in it
Contained by it
But not engaging with it

So detached from it
Sometimes forgetting
That it needs care
...
And it does need care

Living solely between
thought and spirit

Exercising mind and spirit all well and good,
But what about body?
Feeding the mind and soul healthily and in good portions,
All well and good – what about body?
Relaxing the mind from intense work
Meditating for the soul
Yet, where's the resting for the carrier?

Loving and grateful towards
Intelligence and spiritual freedom and strength
But hating the capsule in the Life dimension,
It's not true love of self

Seek to take care of all three
You ARE a trinity being.

Printed in Great Britain
by Amazon

42642540R00020